• MUSIC •

Pop and Rock

Nicolas Brasch

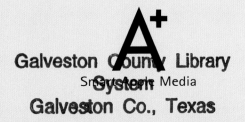

Smart Apple Media

Smart Apple Media
1980 Lookout Drive
North Mankato
Minnesota 56003

Library of Congress Cataloging-in-Publication Data

Brasch, Nicolas.
    Pop and rock music / by Nicolas Brasch.
    p. cm. — (Music)
    Includes index.
    ISBN 1-58340-546-1 (alk. paper)
    1. Popular music—History and criticism—Juvenile literature. 2. Rock music—History and criticism—Juvenile literature. I. Title.

    ML3470.B735 2004
    781.64—dc22   2004041600

First Edition
9 8 7 6 5 4 3 2 1

First published in 2003 by
MACMILLAN EDUCATION AUSTRALIA PTY LTD
627 Chapel Street, South Yarra 3141

Associated companies and representatives throughout the world.

Copyright © Nicolas Brasch 2003

Project management by Elm Grove Press
Edited by Helen Duffy
Text design by Judith Summerfeldt Grace
Cover design by Judith Summerfeldt Grace
Photo research by Helen Duffy and Ingrid Ohlsson

Printed in China

Acknowledgements
The author and the publisher are grateful to the following for permission to reproduce copyright material.

Cover photographs: Photodisc (musical instruments); Bruce Postle (left, the Rolling Stones); Redferns Music Picture Library/All Action (right, Madonna).

Text photographs: John Lamb, p. 22 (ABBA female vocalists); PhotoAlto, p. 3 (bottom); Photodisc, pp. 1 (center), 7 (musical notes), 9 (musical notes), 11 (musical notes), 12 (musical notes), 13 (musical notes), 14 (musical instruments), 15 (musical instruments); Bruce Postle, pp. 1 (left, Cyndi Lauper), 1 (right, Billy Joel in concert), 3 (top, guitarist, Savage Garden), 3 (second top, pianist, Ted Vining Trio, Melbourne Jazz Festival, 2003), 3 (third top, New Zealand's Ortiz Funeral Directors jazz band, Melbourne Jazz Festival, 2003), 4 (from the collection in the Louvre, Paris), 5 (pianist, Ted Vining Trio, Melbourne Jazz Festival, 2003), 8 (Cliff Richard), 9 (The Rolling Stones), 12 (Cyndi Lauper), 14 (left, Bo Diddley), 16 (Johnny O'Keefe, Brisbane Festival Hall, 1958), 17 (left, David Bowie), 17 (right, Bob Dylan), 20 (The Beatles, Brisbane Festival Hall, 1964), 21 (The Rolling Stones on tour in the 1990s), 24 (Chuck Berry), 25 (scene from *Buddy*), 26 (The Easybeats), 27 (Elton John); Sandy Scheltema, p. 18 (Michael Jackson); Redferns Music Picture Library, pp. 7 (copyright Michael Ochs Archives/Redferns), 10 (copyright Keith Morris/Redferns), 11 (copyright Richard E. Aaron/Redferns), 19 (copyright All Action/Redferns), 23 (copyright Richard E. Aaron/Redferns), 28 (copyright Michael Ochs Archives/Redferns), 29 (copyright Mick Hutson/Redferns), 30 (copyright Mick Hutson/Redferns).

While every care has been taken to trace and acknowledge copyright, the publisher tenders their apologies for any accidental infringement where copyright has proved untraceable. Where the attempt has been unsuccessful, the publisher welcomes information that would redress the situation.

Contents

Glossary
When a word is printed in **bold** you can find its meaning in the Glossary on page 31.

Understanding Music

Music has been enjoyed since ancient times.

Music is the arrangement and performance of a combination of sounds that are created by the human voice or by instruments. The ability to turn sounds into music or to create sounds that do not come naturally is something that only humans can do.

The desire to make music is common among all people. It helps us to communicate ideas or emotions and to understand our surroundings and way of life, as well as that of others.

Since ancient times, even isolated communities developed their own forms of music. Different groups used different techniques and instruments to create their own musical sounds.

Music is a creative art form. It also plays an important role in other art forms. Dance and some forms of theater use music to support the action on stage and to help create mood. Music also helps to create atmosphere in films and many television programs.

Music has its own written language, or **score**, made up of symbols and notes. Different musical notes are used to indicate the length of a sound. Notes are represented by the letters A, B, C, D, E, F, and G. These letters or notes are marked on a stave, which is a set of five parallel lines. The position of a note on the stave indicates whether the note is high or low.

Some of the most well-known types of music are:

- classical
- opera
- jazz
- blues
- folk
- country
- reggae
- pop
- rock

This book is about pop and rock music.

Main Elements of Music

The main elements of all music are:

dynamics   the variation in volume (from loud to soft)

pitch   the depth of a sound (whether it is "high" or "low")

rhythm   the general pattern or movement of a piece of music, which is created by the length of time between each beat

timbre   the tonal quality of a sound

tonality   the use of keys in music

Important Musical Terms

chord   a combination of two or more musical notes played at the same time

harmony   a specific chord or a series of chords

melody   a series of musical sounds of different pitch (when you hum the tune of a song, you are usually humming the melody)

texture   the thickness of a sound

Pop and Rock Music

Pop and rock music developed in the 1950s and 1960s and became the most popular music for young people.

Pop Music

The term "pop" has been used since the late 1950s to describe the best-known, most successful kinds of popular music. At this time, improvements in technology made records widely available, and radio and television programs promoted performers, further increasing music sales. In the 1950s and 1960s, pop music focused on teenage themes, such as boy-girl relationships, weekend activities, clothes, and cars. It was usually music with a simple rhythm, and the popularity of songs often lasted only a short time.

Rock and Roll Music

Rock music developed from rock and roll music, a form of popular music that developed in the United States in the 1950s. Rock and roll grew out of earlier types of music, including **blues**, **rhythm and blues**, **gospel music**, **country and western**, and early pop. Blues, rhythm and blues, and gospel music were played by African-Americans in the United States, and country and western and pop were played and sung by non-African American artists. Rock and roll featured a loud and heavy rhythm, and started a dance craze that further increased its popularity.

Rock Music

In the 1960s, rock and roll was influenced by British performers, in particular the Beatles. From this time, the music became known simply as "rock." It focused on youth protest, lifestyle, and drugs. Its **lyrics**, or words, are written to appeal to teenagers, it has a regular beat and amplified singing and electric instruments. From the 1970s, rock has had many forms and includes everything from punk and heavy metal to hip-hop and rap.

History of Pop and Rock Music

Stars of the Early Pop Era

Rudy Vallee (1901–1986)

Guy Lombardo (1902–1977)

Bing Crosby (1904–1977)

Frank Sinatra (1915–1998)

Peggy Lee (1920–2002)

Judy Garland (1922–1969)

Doris Day (born in 1924)

Tony Bennett (born in 1926)

Johnny Ray (1927–1990)

Guy Mitchell (1927–1999)

Hits of the Early Pop Era

"Swanee" (1919) Bing Crosby

"Yes We Have No Bananas" (1923) Billy Jones

"Star Dust" (1928) Hoagy Carmichael

"Night and Day" (1932) Fred Astaire

"Over the Rainbow" (1939) Judy Garland

"White Christmas" (1941) Bing Crosby

"Stormy Weather" (1943) Lena Horne

"Cry" (1951) Johnny Ray

"Que Sera Sera" (1956) Doris Day

The timeline, below right, gives some important pop and rock events of the 1950s.

Pop and Rock Stars of the 1950s

Chuck Berry (born in 1926)

Little Richard (born in 1932)

Jerry Lee Lewis (born in 1935)

Elvis Presley (1935–1977)

Gene Vincent (1935–1971)

Buddy Holly (1936–1959)

Eddie Cochran (1938–1960)

Connie Francis (born in 1938)

Bill Haley and the Comets (group formed in 1949)

The Platters (group formed in 1953)

Although the term "pop" was not used until the 1950s, its history dates back to the late 1800s. Music publishing companies hired songwriters to compose short, catchy tunes, and sold sheet music containing the music and words. Sheet music had wide appeal because it enabled people to play the music on the piano and sing along at home. The United States was the largest market for this early form of popular music. The area in New York City where most of the publishers were based became known as Tin Pan Alley.

Early 1900s

In the early 1900s, record players became popular and radio technology improved. People could listen to records at home or on the radio. The success of popular music was measured by record sales, rather than sheet music sales.

The earliest forms of popular music were heavily influenced by **opera**. Songs from operas were published or recorded and became hits in their own right. Other influences were theatrical musical comedies and **jazz**.

The period immediately after World War II was a boom time for popular music in the United States. Young people were confident about their future and happy to spend money on entertainment. Record companies signed up recording artists in the hope of finding the next big hit.

1950	1951	1952	1953	1954
	During 1950-51, the term "rock and roll" is used for the first time by American disc jockey Alan Freed	In March, Alan Freed puts on the first of many rock and roll concerts		In July, Elvis Presley makes his first recordings at Sun Records

The 1950s

Popular music changed dramatically in the 1950s. The light, melodic sounds were replaced by louder, faster sounds. This music was named rock and roll, and it was a form of music that teenagers made their own. The music defined a whole generation and performers were idolized.

The Role of Rhythm and Blues

Rock and roll music was heavily influenced by rhythm and blues. Rhythm and blues was one of the first forms of music to feature the electric guitar as the main instrument. It was first played in the United States by African-Americans. However, at the beginning of the 1950s, some non-African American musicians began playing and singing rhythm and blues. They changed the style a little, making it louder and wilder. Rock and roll music was born.

First Rock and Roll Hits

The huge success of two songs ensured the future of rock and roll. Those songs were Bill Haley and the Comets' "Rock Around the Clock" in 1955, and Elvis Presley's "Heartbreak Hotel" in 1956. "Rock Around the Clock" sold 25 million copies and became the first rock and roll song to reach the No. 1 spot on the record charts. When these two songs proved smash hits, record companies quickly signed up performers who sang and played the new, wild style.

The pop artists who had topped the music charts for years found that they were no longer so popular. Some never regained popularity. Others, such as Frank Sinatra, had to wait many years before becoming popular again.

Elvis Presley's recording career lasted from 1954 to 1977. His music had an enormous influence on pop and rock stars who followed. Many combined elements of his music style with their own.

1955	*1956*	*1957*	*1958*	*1959*
In July, "Rock around the Clock" reaches No. 1 on the American record charts	In April, Presley's "Heartbreak Hotel" reaches No. 1 on the American record charts	In February, Bill Haley and the Comets arrive in Britain for a concert tour	In March, Buddy Holly and the Crickets arrive in Britain for a concert tour	
In November, Elvis Presley signs a recording contract with RCA Victor			In February, Buddy Holly, Ritchie Valens, and the Big Bopper are killed in a plane crash	

Hits of the 1950s

"Rock Around the Clock" (1955) Bill Haley and the Comets
"Heartbreak Hotel" (1955) Elvis Presley
"That'll be the Day" (1955) Buddy Holly and the Crickets
"Blueberry Hill" (1956) Fats Domino
"Jailhouse Rock" (1957) Elvis Presley
"Johnny B Goode" (1958) Chuck Berry
"Living Doll" (1959) Cliff Richard

The 1960s

By the early 1960s, rock and roll music in the United States was losing some of its appeal. The loud, wild sound no longer seemed as new and exciting as it had a few years earlier. Young people were looking for a different music sound. This was to come from across the other side of the Atlantic Ocean, from Britain.

The British Beat

American rock and roll records, and tours of Britain by groups such as Bill Haley and the Comets, and Buddy Holly and the Crickets, inspired many young people in Britain to have a go themselves. At first they copied the American music, but a different sound soon began to emerge. This became known as the British beat. It was less frenzied than the American rock and roll and contained more elements of the original early pop music. It became known simply as rock music. By 1964, British acts were touring the United States, influencing the youth of America. The band that proved the biggest success was the Beatles.

Motown Saves the Day

Pop made a comeback in the United States in the 1960s, mainly through one record company, Motown, founded in 1959. Based in the city of Detroit, Motown produced hit after hit. Most performers were African-American and they sang three-minute songs about love. They were perfect pop songs. Motown was largely responsible for saving the American pop and rock industry and started the careers of future superstars such as Michael Jackson, Diana Ross, and Stevie Wonder.

England's Cliff Richard released his first single in 1958 and had many hits in the 1960s. He still tours and performs worldwide and is one of the pop era's greatest stars.

The timeline, below right, gives some important pop and rock events of the 1960s.

Pop and Rock Stars of the 1960s

Bob Dylan (born in 1941)
Jimi Hendrix (1942–1970)
Stevie Wonder (born in 1950)
The Beatles (group formed in 1957)
The Supremes (group formed in 1959)
The Beach Boys (group formed in 1961)
The Rolling Stones (group formed in 1962)
The Jackson 5 (group formed in 1963)
The Who (group formed in 1964)
The Doors (group formed in 1965)

1960	*1961*	*1962*	*1964*
Elvis Presley returns to the music scene after two years service in the army	In December, the Motown record label has its first No. 1 hit record on the music charts	In January, the Beatles have their first No. 1 hit record	In February, the Beatles arrive in the United States for a concert tour

In April, the Beatles hold the top five places on the U.S. charts |

San Francisco, California

By the late 1960s, California had become the center of the music world. Thousands of hippies from all over the United States, and from Europe, moved to San Francisco. They favored songs about peace and love, and organized big outdoor concerts. The largest concert was Woodstock, held on a farm in 1969. It was attended by more than half a million people.

The Rolling Stones were an English group, formed in 1962. They were considered more rebellious than their rivals, the Beatles. Photographed here in Australia in the mid-1960s were band members, left to right, Mick Jagger, Brian Jones (died 1969), and Keith Richards.

1965	1966	1967	1969
In July, Bob Dylan outrages the audience at the Newport Folk Festival by playing the electric guitar	In August, the Beatles make their last concert appearance, at Candlestick Park in San Francisco	In June, the first major outdoor rock concert is held at Monterey in California	In August, Woodstock outdoor rock festival is held

Hits of the 1960s

"The Twist" (1960) Bill Haley and the Comets
"Crying" (1961) Roy Orbison
"Where Did Our Love Go" (1964) The Supremes
"House of the Rising Sun" (1964) The Animals
"You Really Got Me" (1964) The Kinks
"(I Can't Get No) Satisfaction" (1965) The Rolling Stones
"Good Vibrations" (1966) The Beach Boys
"Hey Jude" (1968) The Beatles
"Heard it Through the Grapevine" (1968) Marvin Gaye
"All Along the Watchtower" (1968) Jimi Hendrix

The 1970s

By the end of the 1960s, the heavy sound of rock was once again gradually replacing the more gentle sound of pop. The hippie culture of peace and love also faded, particularly after a concertgoer was killed by members of the Hells Angels motorcycle gang at an outdoor Rolling Stones concert, held in December 1969.

Heavy Metal

The loudest, rawest rock sound of the early 1970s was heavy metal. It was characterized by long songs that were only starting to warm up after three minutes, which was the total duration of traditional pop songs. These heavy metal songs often featured lengthy, loud electric guitar and drum solos, and screaming singers. Major stars of heavy metal were Black Sabbath, Deep Purple, Iron Maiden, Led Zeppelin, Thin Lizzy, Aerosmith, Maidenhead, AC/DC, and Alice Cooper.

Glam Rock

Glam rock incorporated elements of both pop and heavy metal. Glam rock songs had more melody than heavy metal songs but still relied on a heavy electric guitar and drum sound. Another feature of glam rock was the theatrical costumes and make-up worn by the artists. Glam rock was launched by David Bowie. He was followed by other stars such as T-Rex, Gary Glitter, Alvin Stardust, The Sweet, Suzi Quatro, Slade, Skyhooks, Mott the Hopple, Mud, Roxy Music, Cockney Rebel, and New York Dolls.

Marc Bolan was a rock and roller and hippie before he joined the glam rock movement with group T-Rex.

The timeline, below right, gives some important pop and rock events of the 1970s.

Rock and Pop Stars of the 1970s

Rod Stewart (born in 1945)
David Bowie (born in 1947)
Elton John (born in 1947)
The Bee Gees (group formed in 1958)
Bay City Rollers (group formed in 1967)
Led Zeppelin (group formed in 1968)
ABBA (group formed in 1971)
The Eagles (group formed in 1971)
Paul McCartney and Wings (group formed in 1971)
The Sex Pistols (group formed in 1975)

1970	1971	1972	1973
In April, the Beatles break up	Death of Jim Morrison, lead singer of the Doors	David Bowie releases his album *The Rise and Fall of Ziggy Stardust*, to launch the glam rock movement	In February, Elton John has his first No.1 hit song with "Crocodile Rock"

Punk

In 1976, the punk movement revived the rebellion and aggression of early rock. Its style of dress and behaviour was a reaction against the luxurious lifestyles of the glam rock and heavy metal rock stars. The idea of punk was that anyone could take part. The sound did not have to be particularly musical. It just had to have passion. Britain was the center of the punk movement. The stars of this period were the Sex Pistols, the Clash, Stiff Little Fingers, the Saints, the Buzzcocks, the Damned, Sham 69, the Dead Kennedys, Generation X, X-Ray Spex, and the Jam.

Disco

While punk was proving a force in Britain, disco was having the same effect in the United States. The one purpose of disco music was to make people dance. Drum machines and synthesizers were often used to provide the regular, hypnotic beat. The disco craze was given a boost by the release of the hit film *Saturday Night Fever*, featuring the music of the Bee Gees. Other disco stars were Chic, Donna Summer, Michael Jackson, Thelma Houston, Gloria Gaynor, KC & the Sunshine Band, and Boney M.

Traditional Pop

Throughout all the different musical movements of the 1970s, traditional pop singers and groups remained an important part of popular music, regularly topping the record charts. Among the most successful were a Scottish band, the Bay City Rollers, and a Swedish band, ABBA.

The Bee Gees were brothers, born in England but raised in Australia. Their early style copied the Beatles, but they soon developed a very distinctive sound of their own.

1975	1976	1977	1979
In 1975, Queen produces the first elaborate video to help sell "Bohemian Rhapsody," which reaches No.1	The Bee Gees' album *Saturday Night Fever* helps make disco the top sound in the United States	In April, ABBA have their first No.1 hit in the United States with "Dancing Queen"	Eleven people are killed during a crush at a concert by The Who
In November, first live performance by the Sex Pistols		In August, Elvis Presley dies	

Hits of the 1970s

"Bridge Over Troubled Water" (1970)
   Simon and Garfunkel
"Big Yellow Taxi" (1970) Joni Mitchell
"American Pie" (1972) Don McLean
"Goodbye Yellow Brick Road" (1973) Elton John
"Piano Man" (1974) Billy Joel
"Mamma Mia" (1975) ABBA
"Hotel California" (1977) The Eagles
"Stayin' Alive" (1978) The Bee Gees
"Rapper's Delight" (1979) Sugarhill Gang

Cyndi Lauper was one of the many female rock and pop stars of the 1980s.

The timeline, below right, gives some important pop and rock events of the 1980s, 1990s, and beyond 2000.

Pop and Rock Stars of the 1980s

Michael Jackson (born in 1958)
Madonna (born in 1958)
Prince (born in 1958)
U2 (group formed in 1976)
Duran Duran (group formed in 1978)
Spandau Ballet (group formed in 1979)
REM (group formed in 1980)

Hits of the 1980s

"Do You Really Want to Hurt Me" (1982)
    Culture Club
"Billie Jean" (1983) Michael Jackson
"Like a Virgin" (1985) Madonna
"Graceland" (1985) Paul Simon
"Faith" (1987) George Michael
"The Wind Beneath My Wings" (1989) Bette Midler

The 1980s

The 1980s saw the birth of new sounds and it also saw the rise of women artists in the pop and rock music world.

Rap

In the early 1980s, a new beat known as rap became popular, particularly on the streets. While the lyrics of disco had been less important than the beat, the lyrics in rap music often had a political or social message. Rap singers were known as rappers and they talked or chanted, rather than sang. Rap became particularly popular among young African-Americans in the United States.

The New Romantics

The new romantic movement began in Britain and had a very distinctive dance beat. However, it was fashion that dominated this movement. Male and female performers and followers dressed up in expensive, frilly, lacy outfits. The most popular new romantic bands were Duran Duran, Spandau Ballet, and Flock of Seagulls.

Women Performers

Cyndi Lauper's hit single "Girls Just Want to Have Fun" summed up the 1980s. More and more young women wanted to get a taste of pop and rock stardom. Some became **solo** performers, others formed bands, such as Bananarama, a British all-girl group that had several hit singles. The biggest female superstar of the 1980s was Madonna. Her songs and live shows set out to prove to the male-dominated music industry that anything boys can do, girls can do better.

1980	1982	1983	1984	1985	1987
In December, former Beatle John Lennon is murdered	Michael Jackson's *Thriller* becomes the biggest-selling album of all time		In December, Madonna has her first hit single with "Like a Virgin"	In July, Live Aid concert is held in London to raise money for drought relief in Ethiopia	The Rolling Stones celebrate 25 years together

CDs first appear on the market and are set to take over from vinyl records as the most popular form of recording

The 1990s

The rap of the 1980s developed into a range of other music styles in the 1990s, including hip-hop.

Hip-hop

Hip-hop was a movement that combined rap, **deejaying**, **breakdance**, and graffiti art.

Grunge

In the early 1990s, a new rock movement began in Seattle in the United States. It was influenced by both punk and heavy metal and was led by the band Nirvana. This was "grunge-rock," which had the passion and volume of punk and heavy metal but also had the melody that these lacked. The success of grunge caused record companies to sign up lots of grunge bands in the hope of finding a winner.

Techno

Techno is also known as house or dance music. Disc jockeys replaced live musicians in many clubs and other music venues. They set up huge sound systems and played music that was a mixture of music recorded by others. The result was a loud, persistent, pounding rhythm that fans danced to for hours on end.

Pop

Pop in the later 1990s was characterized by the popularity of girl and boy groups. These groups were formed by record companies, who provided them with songs and extensive marketing. The most popular girl group was the Spice Girls, while the most popular boy group was Take That.

Pop and Rock Beyond 2000

Since the end of the 1990s, no single music form has dominated the rock and pop music scene. It now has something for everyone.

- Dance fans flock to clubs to dance to their favorite music.
- Rock fans pack stadiums to hear their favorite artists.
- Pop fans watch cable television shows to catch their teenage idols.
- Heavy metal fans surf the Web to exchange and download sounds from bands all over the world.
- Superstars from the past, such as the Rolling Stones, perform sell-out concerts on world tours.

Pop and Rock Stars of the 1990s and Beyond 2000

Puff Daddy (born in 1970)
Snoop Doggy Dogg (born in 1972)
Eminem (born in 1974)
Boyz II Men (group formed in 1988)
Nirvana (group formed in 1988)
Take That (group formed in 1990)
Pearl Jam (group formed in 1991)
Spice Girls (group formed in 1994)

Hits of the 1990s and Beyond 2000

"One Sweet Day" (1995) Mariah Carey and Boyz II Men
"Candle in the Wind 1997" (1997) Elton John
"Wannabe" (1997) The Spice Girls
"Say My Name" (2000) Destiny's Child
"Can't Get You Out of My Head" (2001) Kylie Minogue

1990	1992	1994	1997	2000
In July, Pink Floyd performs near the site of the former Berlin Wall, soon after it had been torn down	In February, U2 begins two-year world tour		In September, Elton John's tribute to Princess Diana, "Candle in the Wind 1997" is biggest-selling single of all time	
	In April, Nirvana's Kurt Cobain commits suicide		Napster file-sharing technology threatens the future of CD sales; music industry wins court case against Napster in 2000	

Instruments of Pop and Rock Music

Guitar Legends

Chet Atkins (1924–2001)

Chuck Berry (born in 1926)

Bo Diddley (born in 1928)

Scotty Moore (born in 1931)

James Jamerson (1938–1983)

James Burton (born in 1939)

Jimi Hendrix (1942–1970)

Jimmy Page (born in 1944)

Eric Clapton (born in 1945)

Pete Townsend (born in 1945)

Stevie Ray Vaughan (born in 1954)

Eddie Van Halen (born in 1957)

Bo Diddley started recording in 1955 and played everything from ballads to blues. He had a very large collection of guitars, including the unusual square one shown here.

Many instruments have been used in pop and rock music but the most common are electric guitars, drums, keyboards, and synthesizers. Some performers, such as the Beatles and Elton John, have mixed pop and rock music with classical music. Elton John has performed live backed by a full symphony **orchestra**.

Guitars

Most pop and rock songs feature an electric guitar. This instrument had been used earlier in some country, jazz, and blues music, but it particularly suited the loud, pronounced rhythms of rock. The electric guitar differs from an **acoustic** guitar in the way the sound comes out. The sound of an electric guitar travels by wire to an **amplifier**, which projects the sound.

There are three main types of electric guitar. They are:

- lead guitar, which has six strings and plays the melody of a song
- rhythm guitar, which has six strings and plays the rhythm of a song
- bass guitar, which has four strings and plays the **bass** line of a song

Among the most famous rock songs in which the electric guitar features strongly are Jimi Hendrix's "All Along the Watchtower," Eric Clapton's "Layla" and Led Zeppelin's "Stairway to Heaven."

An electric guitar

Drums

Apart from the electric guitar, the next most important **instrumental** section in pop and rock music is the drum kit. Drums provide the singers and other musicians with a song's beat. Without the drums, the other musicians would find it very hard to keep in time. A drum kit usually consists of a bass drum, a snare drum, toms, and cymbals.

In the photograph, the bass drum is the large drum at the front. A pedal operates a **mallet** that beats the drum. The snare drum is the narrow-sided drum on the right at the back. The toms are the two smaller drums suspended above the bass drum, and a floor tom is on the far left.

A drum kit. The instruments that look like large plates are the cymbals: ride cymbal (left); crash cymbal (highest on right); and high hat (below, right), which is pedal-operated. Some cymbals are struck with a stick or wire brush.

Keyboard Instruments

Keyboard instruments include the piano and the keyboard, which is basically an electronic piano. Pianos are rarely included in a band but have been used by a number of solo artists. An exception to this was the Beatles' use of the piano in their song, "Hey Jude." Electric keyboards are often included in a band.

Synthesizer

A synthesizer is a computerized instrument that produces all sorts of sounds. It is usually used to help create a mood, but sometimes the sounds resemble other instruments. The master of the synthesizer was Rick Wakeman, who had several hit **concept albums** in the 1970s. On a concept album, the songs work together to give the album a particular "feel," rather than existing as separate songs.

Other Instruments

Almost every instrument that exists has been used at some time by a rock group. Saxophones and trumpets are particularly common, while violins have also appeared. In 1973, Mike Oldfield released his album *Tubular Bells*, featuring the sounds of different types of bells. It was one of only a few purely instrumental albums to top the charts.

Drum Legends

Earl Palmer (born in 1924)
Hal Blaine (born in 1929)
Ginger Baker (born in 1939)
Charlie Watts (born in 1941)
Keith Moon (1946–1978)
Jon Bonham (1948–1980)

Keyboard Legends

Johnny Johnson (born in 1924)
Ray Charles (born in 1930)
Jerry Lee Lewis (born in 1935)
Elton John (born in 1947)
Billy Joel (born in 1949)

Famous Pop and Rock Performers

Rock fans have always focused on the performer or singer rather than the backing musicians. Often singers are also musicians, usually guitarists, but it is their voices and personalities that make them stars.

Johnny O'Keefe

Johnny O'Keefe

Born January 19, 1935, Sydney, Australia (died October 6, 1978)
Full name John Michael O'Keefe
Hit songs include "You Hit the Wrong Note Billy Goat" (1957), "Shout" (1959), "Sing" (1962), "Move Baby Move" (1963), "Mockingbird" (1974)
Hit albums/CDs include *Johnny's Golden Album* (1959), *Shout* (1960), *Six O'Clock Rock* (1961), *The Johnny O'Keefe Show* (1962)
Profile Australia's first superstar of rock, O'Keefe outperformed the great American artists when they toured Australia.

Elvis Presley

Born January 8, 1935, Tupelo, Mississippi, United States (died August 16, 1977)
Full name Elvis Aaron Presley
Hit songs include "Heartbreak Hotel" (1956), "Don't Be Cruel" (1956), "Love Me Tender" (1956), "Jailhouse Rock" (1957), "Are You Lonesome Tonight" (1960), "Suspicious Minds" (1969)
Hit albums/CDs include *Elvis Presley* (1956), *Loving You* (1957), *G I Blues* (1960), *Blue Hawaii* (1961), *Roustabout* (1964)
Profile Presley was the first superstar of rock. His body movements shocked parents and delighted young fans. Twenty-five years after his death, his songs are still bestsellers.

1986   *1987*

The Rock and Roll Hall of Fame

The Rock and Roll Hall of Fame recognizes the achievements of those involved in the rock and roll industry. Since 1986, several performers have been inducted, or elected, into the Hall of Fame each year.

Chuck Berry	The Everly Brothers
James Brown	Buddy Holly
Ray Charles	Jerry Lee Lewis
Sam Cooke	Elvis Presley
Fats Domino	Little Richard

The Coasters	Ricky Nelson
Eddie Cochran	Roy Orbison
Bo Diddley	Carl Perkins
Aretha Franklin	Smokey Robinson
Marvin Gaye	Big Joe Turner
Bill Haley	Muddy Waters
B. B. King	Jackie Wilson
Clyde McPhatter	

Bob Dylan

Bob Dylan

Born May 24, 1941, Duluth, Minnesota, United States
Full name Robert Allen Zimmerman
Hit songs include "Blowin' in the Wind" (1963),
"The Times They are A-Changin' " (1964), "Mr Tambourine
Man" (1965), "Maggie's Farm" (1965), "Like a Rolling Stone"
(1965), "Lay Lady Lay" (1969)
Hit albums/CDs include *Bob Dylan* (1961), *Freewheelin' Bob Dylan*
(1962), *The Times They are A-Changin'* (1964), *Blonde on Blonde*
(1966), *Self Portrait* (1970)
Profile As a songwriter, singer, and performer, Dylan had a great
influence on young people in the 1960s. His music sparked
protests against the Vietnam War, poverty, and inequality.

David Bowie

Born January 8, 1947, London, England
Full name David Robert Jones
Hit songs include "Space Oddity" (1969), "Changes" (1972),
"Starman" (1972), "Sorrow" (1973), "Fame" (1975),
"Let's Dance" (1983)
Hit albums/CDs include *David Bowie* (1967), *Man of Words,
Man of Music* (1969), *The Man Who Sold the World* (1971),
Aladdin Sane (1973), *Diamond Dogs* (1974)
Profile Bowie started off as a saxophonist before forming his own
band. He was one of the first performers to succeed in combining
pop and rock music with elements of theater.

David Bowie

1988	1989	1990	1991	1992
The Beach Boys	Dion	Hank Ballard	LaVern Baker	Bobby "Blue" Bland
The Beatles	Otis Redding	Bobby Darin	The Byrds	Booker T. and the MGs
The Drifters	The Rolling Stones	The Four Seasons	John Lee Hooker	Johnny Cash
Bob Dylan	The Temptations	The Four Tops	The Impressions	Jimi Hendrix
The Supremes	Stevie Wonder	The Kinks	Wilson Pickett	The Isley Brothers
		The Platters	Jimmy Reed	Sam and Dave
		Simon and Garfunkel	Ike and Tina Turner	The Yardbirds
		The Who		

More Famous Pop and Rock Performers

Elton John

Born March 25, 1947, London, England

Full name Reginald Kenneth Dwight

Hit songs include "Crocodile Rock" (1973), "Bennie and the Jets" (1974), "Philadelphia Freedom" (1975), "Don't Go Breaking My Heart" (with Kiki Dee, 1976), "Healing Hands" (1990), "Candle in the Wind 1997" (1997)

Hit albums/CDs include *Empty Sky* (1969), *Honky Chateau* (1972), *Don't Shoot Me, I'm Only the Piano Player* (1973), *Goodbye Yellow Brick Road* (1973), *Captain Fantastic and the Brown Dirt Cowboy* (1975)

Profile A singer, songwriter, and musician, Elton John has remained at or near the top of the charts for 30 years. At the height of his popularity he was famous for his spectacular concert extravaganzas.

Michael Jackson

Born August 29, 1958, Gary, Indiana, United States

Full name Michael Joseph Jackson

Hit songs include "Ben" (1972), "Don't Stop 'Til You Get Enough" (1979), "Rock with You" (1980), "Billie Jean" (1983), "Beat It" (1983), "Say, Say, Say" (with Paul McCartney, 1983)

Hit albums/CDs include *Off the Wall* (1979), *Thriller* (1982), *Bad* (1987), *Dangerous* (1991), *HIStory: Past Present & Future* (1995)

Profile Jackson, a child star in the Jackson 5, went on to become music's biggest superstar of the 1980s. Since the mid-1990s, his unusual behavior and regular facelifts have made more news than his music.

Michael Jackson

The performers listed below were inducted into the Rock and Roll Hall of Fame between 1993 and 2003.

1993	1994	1995	1996	1997
Ruth Brown	The Animals	The Allman Brothers Band	David Bowie	The Bee Gees
Cream	The Band	Al Green	Gladys Knight and the Pips	Buffalo Springfield
Creedence Clearwater Revival	Duane Eddy	Janis Joplin	Jefferson Airplane	Crosby, Stills, and Nash
The Doors	The Grateful Dead	Led Zeppelin	Little Willie John	The Jackson 5
Frankie Lymon and the Teenagers	Elton John	Martha and the Vandellas	Pink Floyd	Joni Mitchell
Etta James	John Lennon	Neil Young	The Shirelles	Parliament-Funkadelic
Van Morrison	Bob Marley	Frank Zappa	The Velvet Underground	The (Young) Rascals
Sly and the Family Stone	Rod Stewart			

Madonna

Prince

Born June 7, 1958, Minneapolis, Minnesota, United States
Full name Prince Rogers Nelson
Hit songs include "1999" (1982), "Little Red Corvette" (1982), "When Doves Cry" (1984), "Purple Rain" (1984), "Let's Go Crazy" (1984), "Kiss" (1986), "Batdance" (1989)
Hit albums/CDs include *Controversy* (1981), *1999* (1982), *Purple Rain* (1984), *Parade* (1986), *Batman* (1989)
Profile Prince is a songwriter, singer, guitarist, pianist, horn player, and extraordinary dancer. He often mixes musical styles. For a while, he was known by a particular symbol, but he has since reverted to the name of Prince.

Madonna

Born August 16, 1958, Bay City, Michigan, United States
Full name Madonna Louise Ciccone
Hit songs include "Like a Virgin" (1984), "Into the Groove" (1985), "Crazy for You" (1985), "Like a Prayer" (1989), "Vogue" (1990), "Justify My Love" (1991), "Take a Bow" (1995)
Hit albums/CDs include *Madonna* (1983), *Like a Virgin* (1984), *True Blue* (1986), *You Can Dance* (1987), *Like a Prayer* (1989), *Erotica* (1992), *Music* (2000)
Profile Madonna is one of the most successful females of pop and rock. Early in her career she enjoyed shocking audiences, but her success was due to the quality of her songs. She is one of the few music performers to succeed as a film actress.

1998	1999	2000	2001	2002	2003
The Eagles	Billy Joel	Eric Clapton	Aerosmith	Isaac Hayes	AC/DC
Fleetwood Mac	Curtis Mayfield	Earth, Wind & Fire	Solomon Burke	Brenda Lee	The Clash
The Mamas and the Papas	Paul McCartney	Lovin' Spoonful	The Flamingos	Tom Petty and the Heartbreakers	Elvis Costello and the Attractions
Lloyd Price	Del Shannon	The Moonglows	Michael Jackson	Gene Pitney	The Police
Santana	Dusty Springfield	Bonnie Raitt	Queen	Ramones	The Righteous Brothers
Gene Vincent	Bruce Springsteen	James Taylor	Paul Simon	Talking Heads	
	The Staple Singers		Steely Dan		
			Ritchie Valens		

Famous Pop and Rock Groups

When rock and roll started in the mid-1950s, the focus was on the lead singer, rather than the backing musicians. During the 1960s, groups became more popular. The Motown record label started the trend of forming groups to record songs already written. The most famous manufactured group was the Monkees, formed in 1966 to star in a television series.

The Beatles performed in Australia in 1964.

The Beatles

Year formed/current status 1957 (disbanded 1970)
Previous names The Quarrymen, Johnny & the Moondogs, The Rainbows, The Silver Beatles
Original members John Lennon (guitar and vocals), Paul McCartney (guitar and vocals), George Harrison (guitar), Stu Sutcliffe (bass guitar), Pete Best (drums)
Line-up changes Stu Sutcliffe left in 1961 and Paul McCartney took up the role of bass guitarist. Ringo Starr replaced Pete Best in 1962.
Hit songs include "Please, Please Me" (1963), "Can't Buy Me Love" (1964), "I Want To Hold Your Hand" (1964), "Yesterday" (1965), "Hey Jude" (1968), "Get Back" (1969)
Hit albums/CDs include *Help* (1965), *Sgt. Pepper's Lonely Hearts Club Band* (1967), *White Album* (1968), *Abbey Road* (1969), *Let it Be* (1970)
Profile The Beatles are considered the most influential group in the pop and rock music industry because so many other musicians copied their style. Even today, many bands name the Beatles as a major influence on their music.

The Rolling Stones

Year formed/current status 1962 (still performing)
Original members Mick Jagger (vocals), Keith Richards (guitar), Brian Jones (guitar), Dick Taylor (bass guitar), Mick Avory (drums), Ian Stewart (keyboards)
Line-up changes Tony Chapman replaced Mick Avory in late 1962, then Charlie Watts replaced Tony Chapman in 1963. Bill Wyman replaced Dick Taylor in late 1962. Mick Taylor replaced Brian Jones in 1969, after Jones's death. Ronnie Woods replaced Mick Taylor in 1974.
Hit songs include "(I Can't Get No) Satisfaction" (1965), "Get Off My Cloud" (1965), "Paint it Black" (1966), "Ruby Tuesday" (1967), "Honky Tonk Women" (1969)
Hit albums/CDs include *Beggars Banquet* (1968), *Let it Bleed* (1969), *Sticky Fingers* (1971), *Goats Head Soup* (1973), *Some Girls* (1978)
Profile The Rolling Stones is one of rock music's longest-surviving groups, and the lead singer, Mick Jagger, is one of its biggest superstars.

The Beach Boys

Year formed/current status 1961 (still performing)
Previous names Kenny and the Cadets, Carl and the Passions, The Pendletones
Original members Brian Wilson (vocals, keyboards, guitar, bass guitar), Carl Wilson (vocals, keyboards, guitar), Dennis Wilson (vocals, drums), Mike Love (vocals), Al Jardine (vocals, guitar)
Line-up changes David Marks replaced Al Jardine in 1962–1963, then Jardine returned.
Hit songs include "Surfin' Safari" (1962), "Surfin' USA" (1962), "I Get Around" (1964), "Help Me Rhonda" (1965), "Good Vibrations" (1966)
Hit albums/CDs include *Surfin' Safari* (1962), *Beach Boys Party!* (1965), *Pet Sounds* (1966), *The Beach Boys Love You* (1977)
Profile Few bands have produced as many "near perfect" pop songs as the Beach Boys. As a singer-songwriter, Brian Wilson is considered to be a genius.

The Rolling Stones are, left to right, Charlie Watts, Keith Richards, Mick Jagger, and Ronnie Woods.

More Famous Pop and Rock Groups

The Supremes

Year formed/current status 1959 (disbanded 1978)
Previous names The Primettes
Original members Diana Ross (vocals), Florence Ballard (vocals), Mary Wilson (vocals)
Line-up changes Cindy Birdsong replaced Florence Ballard in 1967 and the group was renamed Diana Ross and the Supremes. Jean Terrell replaced Diana Ross in 1970 and the group became the Supremes.
Hit songs include "Where Did Our Love Go" (1964), "Baby Love" (1964), "Stop! In the Name of Love" (1965), "You Can't Hurry Love" (1966), "Someday We'll be Together" (1969)
Hit albums/CDs include *Meet the Supremes* (1963), *Where Did Our Love Go* (1964), *More Hits by the Supremes* (1965), *Supremes a Go Go* (1966)
Profile This was the first all-girl group to sell a million records. The original group line-up was the most successful. Diana Ross went on to have a very successful solo career.

ABBA

Year formed/current status 1972 (disbanded 1982)
Previous names Björn & Benny and Svenska & Flicka
Original members Björn Ulvaeus (vocals, guitar), Benny Andersson (keyboards, vocals), Anni-Frid Lyngstad (vocals), Agnetha Fältskog (vocals)
Hit songs include "Waterloo" (1974), "I Do, I Do, I Do" (1975), "Mamma Mia" (1976), "Fernando" (1976), "Dancing Queen" (1977)
Hit albums/CDs include *ABBA* (1975), *Greatest Hits* (1976), *Arrival* (1976), *The Singles* (1982)
Profile ABBA is the world's most successful pop group from outside the United States and Britain. Their songs made a comeback in the late 1990s.

The ABBA female vocalists were, left to right, Agnetha Fältskog and Anni-Frid Lyngstad.

The Sex Pistols

Year formed/current status 1975 (disbanded 1978)
Original members Johnny Rotten (vocals), Steve Jones (guitar), Paul Cook (drums), Glen Matlock (bass guitar)
Line-up changes Sid Vicious replaced Glen Matlock in 1977.
Hit songs include "Anarchy in the UK" (1976), "God Save the Queen" (1977), "Pretty Vacant" (1977), "Holidays in the Sun" (1977).
Hit albums/CDs include
Never Mind the Bollocks (1977),
The Great Rock and Roll Swindle (1979)
Profile For a group that lasted less than three years, the Sex Pistols had an amazing influence. They shocked audiences, but showed that anyone could play in a rock band and many groups followed their example.

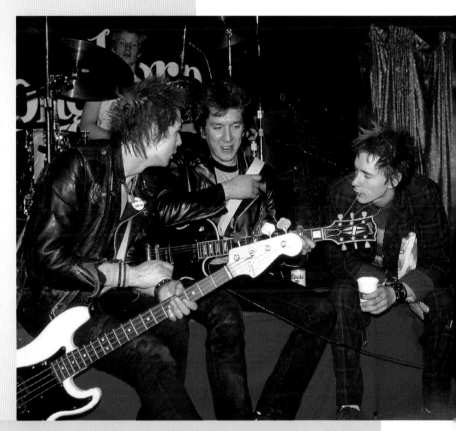

The Sex Pistols

REM

Year formed/current status 1980 (still performing)
Original members Michael Stipe (vocals), Peter Buck (guitar), Bill Berry (drums), Michael Mills (bass guitar)
Line-up changes Bill Berry left in 1997 but has not been permanently replaced.
Hit songs include "The One I Love" (1987), "Pop Song" (1989), "Shiny Happy People" (1991), "Losing My Religion" (1991), "Everybody Hurts" (1993)
Hit albums/CDs include *Murmur* (1983), *Reckoning* (1984), *Document No. 5* (1987), *Green* (1988), *Automatic for the People* (1992)
Profile REM was the biggest band in the late 1980s. They fought hard for **artistic freedom**, insisting on total control over their music before signing with a major record company.

Famous Pop and Rock Compositions

Songs are released as singles, or as part of an album (long-playing record) or CD. Singles contain one main song that the record company hopes will be played on radio. Traditionally, singles are about three minutes long. When they came out on vinyl records, there was a lesser-known song on the reverse, or "b," side.

Chuck Berry

"Maybelline"

Year released 1955
Writer Chuck Berry
Performer Chuck Berry
Chuck Berry took an old country hit named "Ida Red," rewrote it and turned it into one of the wildest early rock and roll songs. Although Berry had bigger hits later, this song launched his career.

"Rock Around the Clock"

Year released 1955
Writers Max Freedman and Jimmy DeKnight
Performers Bill Haley and the Comets
This was the first major rock and roll hit song. It featured on the soundtrack of *Blackboard Jungle*, a film about rebellious teenagers. The song caused riots in movie theaters and concert halls and sold 25 million copies. It was Bill Haley and the Comets' biggest hit and has been recorded more than 500 times by other artists.

Top 20 Pop and Rock Singles of All Time

This list is based on the number of weeks a song has been No. 1 on the charts in the United States, United Kingdom and Australia.

(Source: *Oz Net Music Chart*)

1. **"I Will Always Love You"** Whitney Houston
2. **"(Everything I Do) I Do It For You"** Bryan Adams
3. **"Hey Jude"** The Beatles
4. **"Candle In The Wind 1997"** Elton John
5. **"Macarena"** Los Del Rio
6. **"I'll Be Missing You"** Puff Daddy & Faith Evans
7. **"Wannabe"** The Spice Girls
8. **"End of The Road"** Boyz II Men

"Heartbreak Hotel"

Year released 1956
Writers Mae Axton, Tommy Durdon, and Elvis Presley
Performer Elvis Presley
This song launched Elvis Presley on the road to stardom and encouraged major record companies to record other rock and roll artists. "Heartbreak Hotel" sold over a million copies.

"That'll be the Day"

Year released 1957
Writers Norman Petty, Buddy Holly, and Jerry Allison
Performers Buddy Holly and the Crickets
This song was not as wild as some of the other rock and roll songs of the time but it was extraordinarily successful. It seemed that Buddy Holly was going to become one of the greats of rock and roll. However, he split with the Crickets after their second hit, "Peggy Sue," and was killed in a plane crash in 1959. His third hit, "It Doesn't Matter Anymore," was released after his death.

This is a scene from the 1990s musical *Buddy*, which portrayed the rise to stardom of Buddy Holly.

9 "It's Now or Never" Elvis Presley

10 "I'd Do Anything for Love" Meatloaf

11 "You're the One That I Want" John Travolta & Olivia Newton-John

12 "Singing The Blues" Guy Mitchell

13 "Are You Lonesome Tonight?" Elvis Presley

14 "My Sweet Lord" George Harrison

15 "Gangsta's Paradise" Coolio

16 "Diana" Paul Anka

17 "I Want to Hold Your Hand" The Beatles

18 "Sixteen Tons" Tennessee Ernie Ford

19 "Black or White" Michael Jackson

20 "I Just Called To Say I Love You" Stevie Wonder

More Famous Pop and Rock Compositions

"Where Did Our Love Go"

Year released 1964
Writers Brian Holland, Lamont Dozier, and Edward Holland
Performers The Supremes
This was the first single for the most successful all-girl group of all time. Although the Motown record label had hit songs before this, the song gave Motown a far wider audience that proved loyal for many years.

"Oh Pretty Woman"

Year released 1964
Writers Roy Orbison and Bill Dees
Performer Roy Orbison
This was Roy Orbison's biggest hit and came at a time when American artists were under pressure from the invasion by British rock stars. In its first ten days on sale, the song sold more copies than any other single in history.

"Friday On My Mind"

Year released 1966
Writers Harry Vanda and George Young
Performers The Easybeats
After several hits in Australia, this was the song that launched the Easybeats on the world pop and rock music scene. It was particularly successful in England. In 2001, the Australian Performing Rights Association named it the best Australian song in the past 75 years.

The Easybeats

"Hey Jude"

Year released 1968
Writer Paul McCartney
Performers The Beatles
McCartney broke the
rules with "Hey Jude,"
writing a hit single that
went for over seven
minutes. It was the first
single the Beatles
recorded for their own
record label, Apple
Records. It was also their
best-selling single.

"I Still Haven't Found What I'm Looking For"

Year released 1987
Writers Bono, the Edge, Adam Clayton, and Larry Mullen
Performers U2
This song was U2's first No. 1 hit in the United States and was the
start of their rise to superstar status. It was the second single from
their award-winning album *The Joshua Tree*, and still features in U2's
live performances.

"Candle in the Wind 1997"

Year released 1997
Writers Elton John and Bernie Taupin
Performer Elton John
This song was first recorded in 1973
as a tribute to the American movie star,
Marilyn Monroe, and was rewritten as a
tribute to Princess Diana, following her
death in 1997. "Candle in the Wind 1997"
has sold more copies than any other
pop or rock single.

Elton John

Famous Pop and Rock Albums/CDs

Long-playing records (known as albums) and CDs usually contain about 12 songs. Double albums and CDs contain twice this number of songs. Triple albums and CDs contain three long-playing records or CDs.

The Beach Boys

Pet Sounds

Year released 1966
Performers The Beach Boys
Tracks "Caroline No," "Wouldn't it be Nice," "You Still Believe in Me," "That's Not Me," "Don't Talk," "I'm Waiting for the Day," "Let's Go Away for a While," "Sloop John B," "God Only Knows," "I Know There's an Answer," "Here Today," "I Just Wasn't Made for These Times," "Pet Sounds"
Profile Many music critics regard *Pet Sounds* as the "most perfect" pop album ever produced. However, the style of the songs, all written by Brian Wilson, were so different from the usual upbeat Beach Boys' songs that the album only reached No. 10 on the US charts.

Top 20 Pop and Rock Albums/CDs of All Time

This list is based on sales in the United States, the world's largest market.

(*Source*: Record Industry Association of America)

1. **Eagles: Their Greatest Hits 1971–1975** The Eagles
2. **Thriller** Michael Jackson
3. **The Wall** Pink Floyd
4. **Led Zeppelin IV** Led Zeppelin
5. **Greatest Hits Volume I & II** Billy Joel
6. **Back In Black** AC/DC
7. **The Beatles** The Beatles
8. **Rumours** Fleetwood Mac

Pink Floyd

Dark Side of the Moon

Year released 1973
Performers Pink Floyd
Tracks "Speak to Me," "Breathe in the Air,"
"On the Run," "Time," "The Great Gig in the Sky,"
"Money," "Us and Them," "Any Colour You Like,"
"Brain Damage," "Eclipse"
Profile This album is the most successful concept
album of all time. The title sums up the dark and
mysterious mood of the songs. *Dark Side of the
Moon* has sold over 28 million copies and was in
the U.S. Top 200 charts for a record 723 weeks.

Sgt. Pepper's Lonely Hearts Club Band

Year released 1967
Performers The Beatles
Tracks "Sgt. Pepper's Lonely Hearts Club Band," "With a Little Help from my Friends,"
"Lucy in the Sky with Diamonds," "Getting Better," "Fixing a Hole," "She's Leaving
Home," "Being for the Benefit of Mr. Kite," "Within You, Without You," "When I'm
Sixty-four," "Lovely Rita," "Good Morning, Good Morning," "A Day in the Life"
Profile This album used production technology not used before in pop and rock music.
It was also the first concept album. In the major music awards in the United States, it
won the highest prize, a **Grammy** Award, for Album of the Year in 1967, and was
No. 1 on the U.S. charts for 16 weeks in a row.

9 **The Bodyguard** Whitney Houston

10 **Boston** Boston

11 **Cracked Rear View** Hootie & The Blowfish

12 **Hotel California** The Eagles

13 **Jagged Little Pill** Alanis Morissette

14 **The Beatles 1967–1970** The Beatles

15 **Appetite for Destruction** Guns 'N Roses

16 **Born in the USA** Bruce Springsteen

17 **Dark Side of the Moon** Pink Floyd

18 **Greatest Hits** Elton John

19 **Physical Graffiti** Led Zeppelin

20 **Saturday Night Fever** Bee Gees

More Famous Pop and Rock Albums/CDs

Never Mind the Bollocks

Year released 1977
Performers The Sex Pistols
Tracks "Holidays in the Sun," "Bodies," "No Feelings," "Liar," "God Save the Queen," "Problems," "Seventeen," "Anarchy in the UK," "Submission," "Pretty Vacant," "New York," "EMI"
Profile The first punk album to reach No. 1 on the charts, *Never Mind the Bollocks* summed up the punk music scene perfectly. It was loud, fast, raw, and exciting. It also went to No. 1 on the British charts. After its success, punk was taken seriously.

Thriller

Year released 1982
Performer Michael Jackson
Tracks "Wanna Be Startin' Something," "Baby Be Mine," "The Girl is Mine," "Thriller," "Beat It," "Billie Jean," "Human Nature," "PYT (Pretty Young Thing)," "The Lady in My Life"
Profile Seven of the songs on this album made it into the Top Ten on the charts and the album was No. 1 on the U.S. album chart for 37 weeks. *Thriller* won the Grammy Award for Album of the Year in 1983, and is the best-selling album of all time, taking into account all the world markets.

Nevermind

Year released 1991
Performers Nirvana
Tracks "Smells Like Teen Spirit," "In Bloom," "Come as You Are," "Breed," "Lithium," "Polly," "Territorial Pissings," "Drain You," "Lounge Act," "Stay Away," "On a Plain," "Something in the Way"
Profile *Nevermind* took Nirvana from being a small-time "garage band" to superstardom, and led to the American city of Seattle becoming the heart of the grunge-rock music scene for the rest of the 1990s. The success of the album took Nirvana by surprise. It sold three million copies and topped the U.S. charts.

Kurt Cobain of Nirvana

Glossary

acoustic   having a sound made naturally, rather than made louder by electronic means

amplifier   device that makes a sound louder by the use of electricity

artistic freedom   freedom to create whatever one wants, without interference or control by others

bass   the lowest part in a piece of music (for an instrument) and the lowest pitch for a male voice

blues   African-American music developed from work songs and characterized by its focus on emotions of sadness

breakdance   form of acrobatic dance, with spectacular movements such as spinning the body on the ground

concept albums   albums in which the songs work together to give the albums a particular "feel," rather than existing as separate songs

country and western   American popular music originating in the southern United States and developed from folk songs and ballads

deejaying   disc jockeys in clubs playing and mixing music

gospel music   emotional form of religious singing common in African-American communities in the southern United States

Grammy   the major music award in the United States

instrumental   piece of music featuring instruments but no voices

jazz   music developed by African-Americans, and characterized by a swinging rhythm

lyrics   the words to a song

mallet   hammer-like tool with a head made of rubber, metal, or wood

opera   stage production in which the characters tell the story by singing

orchestra   large group of people playing different types of instruments, usually string, woodwind, brass, and percussion

rhythm and blues   music developed by African-Americans from the blues

score   written copy of a piece of music

solo   one single performer, or instrument, playing on its own

Index